Smudge and Chewpen Word Book

Paul Groves and Nigel Grimshaw

Edward Arnold

© Paul Groves and Nigel Grimshaw 1980

First published 1980 by
Edward Arnold (Publishers) Ltd
41 Bedford Square
London WC1B 3DQ

British Library Cataloguing in Publication Data
Groves, Paul
  Smudge and Chewpen word book.
  1. Vocabulary — Juvenile literature
  I. Title II. Grimshaw, Nigel
  428'.1   PE1449

ISBN 0-7131-0462-7

Acknowledgements
The Publishers wish to thank the following for permission to reproduce
copyright material:
Mary Borrows (page 88); Jonathan Cape Ltd (page 73); J M Dent & Sons
Ltd (page 73); Faber & Faber (Publishers) Ltd (page 80); Longman Group
Ltd (page 51); Murray Pollinger (pages 43 & 72); The Post Office (page
62); A P Watt Ltd (page 71); the Youth Hostels Association (page 63).

Text set in IBM 11/12 pt Press Roman by 𝍏 Tek-Art, Croydon, Surrey.
Printed in Great Britain by Spottiswoode Ballantyne Limited,
Colchester and London

Contents

To the teacher

It is generally accepted that the best way of increasing your vocabulary is to read widely. In this television age, however, many pupils read very little out of school. This book is an attempt to interest this kind of pupil in words. Using the *Smudge and Chewpen* approach it tells the story of how Jim and Anne increased their vocabulary with a series of varied exercises. The pupil is invited to join with them in doing the exercises. Many of the sections, though, can be used separately with the teacher's own work scheme. The book also invites the pupil to discuss the meanings of words with his teachers and any discussion work that can be done on these lines will repay the teacher handsomely.

Part one

Over-used words

Part One

Over-used words

1

Kind of... sort of... couple of...

Jim Smudge was writing a story:

> I saw this man down the road. He was wearing a sort of black bomber jacket. He had a couple of parcels under his arms. They were probably stolen. He had a funny kind of look about him. I was pretty sure he was up to no good.

'Just a minute, Jim,' said Mr Wright, his English teacher. 'I am sure this is going to be an exciting story but I think it is time we began to improve your English in another way now we have got you writing more accurately.'

'What's up, sir?' asked Jim.

'I want you to be more exact in your English. I want you to pick the right word to describe and explain things. Look at these phrases you have used,' said Mr Wright:

sort of
couple of
funny look
kind of
pretty sure

'What do you mean by a "sort of black bomber jacket"? Do you mean faded black? Jet black? Or do you mean it was not really a bomber jacket but some other jacket? I want you to improve these sentences. Try to avoid over-used, vague expressions.'

Try this with Jim

  (a) The pudding was a sort of yellowy colour.
  (b) I sort of hit him as he came round the corner.
  (c) The coat was a sort of brown colour.

(d) It was an odd sort of game.

(e) It soon became sort of cloudy.

How did you get on? Did you feel you could just leave the imprecise term out? Did you want to use any of the other imprecise phrases from the list?

Now see if you can improve on these:

(f) He had a couple of hours to spare.

(g) I'll be there in a couple of minutes when I've finished making the jam.

(h) She had a couple of children with her.

(i) Let me have a couple of pounds.

(j) I shall come to stay in a couple of days' time.

Funny is correctly used in this sentence: *The joke was very funny.* What do we really mean by funny in these sentences?

(k) Suddenly I felt all funny.

(l) She gave him a funny look.

(m)He was a funny looking man.

(n) The funny part about it was that I was never there.

(o) He got very funny with me, when I told him.

Kind of is used correctly in this sentence: *It was kind of you to let me come.* But can you improve on these sentences?

(p) His hair had a kind of wave in it.

(q) She was wearing a kind of imitation fur coat.

(r) He had a kind of odd look in his eyes.

(s) She looked kind of ill when she saw the accident.

(t) I felt kind of bored as he went on and on.

Pretty is used correctly in the following sentence: *She was a pretty girl.* Now see if you can improve on these sentences:

(u) He was pretty good at cricket.

(v) I am pretty sure he will come.

(w) She did pretty well in the exams.

(x) I was feeling pretty poorly so I did not go.
(y) I thought she looked pretty silly in that hat.

How difficult did you find these sentences to do? Did you need to discuss many with your teacher? If you did, this book can help you a great deal.

2

Nice. . . nice. . . nice. . .

One day Anne Chewpen wrote this:

> She had a nice house with a nice garden. It was in a very nice road. Most of the things in the house were nice. She had nice carpets and the decorations were very nice . . .

'That's very nice, Anne,' said Miss Madd.
'Oh, good!' exclaimed Anne.
'I'm being sarcastic, Anne, I'm afraid,' sighed Miss Madd.
'Why?' asked Anne.
'Just look at the word "nice".'
'I've used it six times.'
'Indeed you have. It's a useful word in speech but in writing it should be used as sparingly as possible. Mr Wright is improving Jim's vocabulary. I think I'd better improve yours. Here is a list of words you could have used instead of "nice" ':

> luxurious   colourful   well-chosen   pleasing   fashionable
> spacious   grand   pleasant   harmonious   tasteful
> attractive   well-designed   grand

'Now write it out again using words from the list.'

How would you have improved Anne's piece of writing? Write your version. When you have finished, exchange with your neighbour. Which is the best version?

Here is another piece for you to do. Words from the list underneath could help you.

> When I went to the seaside I had a very nice time. Luckily it was a nice day. I went with the Jacobs who are very nice

people. They bought me two ice creams which I thought was nice of them. They were very nice ices. It was nice to walk along the sea front. Out in the bay the sea was a nice blue.

creamy   clear   fine   sunny   enjoyable   exciting   gorgeous exhilarating   agreeable   bright   pleasant   friendly generous   invigorating   kind   bracing   tasty   luscious

Now do it again using some or all different words and decide which is the best piece.

Here are some other words you can use instead of *nice*:

delightful   pleasure-giving   pleasurable   congenial   welcome grateful   gratifying   satisfying   amusing

Here are some particularly for *food*:

tempting   appetizing   palatable   dainty   delicate delicious   exquisite   juicy   succulent   rich

Now write about one of these subjects without using *nice*:

The best meal you have eaten
A day at the seaside
Christmas Day

Finally pick ten words from the lists in this section that you do not normally use and write a sentence for each.

3

Got...get...getting...

Mr Wright looked over Jim's shoulder one day. 'What is this, Jim?' he asked.

'It's going to be a great mystery story,' Jim told him.

'Let me read it,' requested Mr Wright.

This is what he read.

When he <u>got back</u>, he got the letter out of the desk and read it again. Had he really <u>got it right</u>? When he had <u>got through</u> it for a second time, he thought for a while. It seemed clear enough. He had also <u>got through</u> what he had been asked to do.

He had <u>got</u> a taxi to the station. He had <u>got</u> there well in time. When the train <u>had got in</u>, he had <u>got</u> the parcel. He had <u>got</u> the parcel to a left luggage office and <u>got</u> a receipt for it. He had <u>got</u> to a letter-box and posted the receipt in the envelope he had <u>got</u>. No one had noticed him. No one had <u>got on his track</u>. He had got rid of the parcel and the receipt. There was nothing now to connect him with Morrison or the crime. Why then was he <u>getting so worried</u>? He did not normally <u>get</u> jittery.

'Well, it's full of mystery,' said Mr Wright, 'but it's also full of something else, as you can see from my underlining.'

'Ah!' said Jim.

' "Got", "get" and "getting",' said Mr Wright. 'They're very useful words in speech but we can sometimes be more varied in writing.'

Here are some words and phrases Jim could have used:

understood it   done   arrived   deposited   returned
took   taken   re-read   followed him   so anxious

been given   walked   came   collected   disposed of
become   received

Replace the underlined words and phrases selecting from the list above. They are not in the right order. You must sort them out.

Here are some more sentences. Either replace the *got, get* **or** *getting* **or rewrite the sentence to avoid these words. These words may help.**

attained   achieved   bored   pay   understand   have   bought
fetch   own   call   communicate   became   hit   obtaining

(a) What a lot I've got!
(b) He got a good result in the exams.
(c) He got me one in the eye with the ball.
(d) I soon got fed up with them.
(e) I don't get the answer.
(f) I'll get him back for that.
(g) I'll go and get her for tea.
(h) That is not as good as the one I've got.
(j) He soon got lost in the mountains.
(k) She got very angry with me.
(l) I could see she was getting conceited.

4

A lot of... a lot of... a lot of...

Jim was writing about the football match last Saturday. He began:

> There were a lot of people at the match last Saturday. I had to find my way through a lot of cars and coaches. There were also a lot of supporters for the visiting team pushing and shoving on the paths. There were a lot of ticket touts at the gates but I had my ticket. Obviously a lot of people had not got one. Mine had cost me a lot of money and I had spent a lot of time queuing, but it was going to be worth it.
>
> When I got inside I had never seen such a lot of policemen. They were obviously expecting a lot of trouble ...

Jim stopped and scratched his head. Mr Wright came and looked over his shoulder.

'I know there's something wrong with this,' said Jim.

'Well, I can tell you one thing,' said Mr Wright. 'It's something that annoys me when I'm marking your work.'

'What is it?' asked Jim.

'A lot of ... a lot of ... a lot of ... ,' said Mr Wright.

'Oh yes!' exclaimed Jim.

'There are ways of avoiding "a lot of". Here are some examples:

many   plenty of   a number of   an enormous number of
numerous   a considerable number of   a great quantity of
an excess of   a mass of   an abundance of   a great deal of
a profusion of   several   much

Perhaps 'many' is one of the best and the most under-used words by my pupils. Sometimes there are special words for 'many'. Do you know these?'

a crowd of people
a herd of cows
a swarm of bees
a gaggle of geese
a pride of lions
a troop of soldiers
a troupe of clowns
a flock of sheep
a flight of starlings
a school of whales
a gang of thieves
a litter of piglets
a pack of hounds
a bevy of beauties
a coven of witches
a board of directors
a band of musicians
a choir of singers
a class of pupils
a crew of sailors
a plague of locusts
a team of players
a staff of teachers
a throng of spectators

Do you know any more?
Sort them into two lists, (a) those that are useful today,
(b) those that are old-fashioned.
Now go back and re-write Jim's piece about the football match.
To avoid *a lot* **these words are useful:**

greatly vastly hugely enormously mightily intensely
immeasurably extremely a great deal frequently

Now improve these sentences. Be careful with (e) and (f).

(a) A lot of the pens did not work.
(b) A lot of birds settled in the telephone wires.
(c) A lot of starlings roosted in the wood.
(d) There are a lot of people who don't like football.
(e) There were a lot of cows in the field.

17

(f) There were a lot of hounds with the huntsman.
(g) It did not help him a lot.
(h) A lot of fish passed the bow of the boat.
(i) He had caused a lot of trouble.
(j) A lot of them did not work.
(k) The sow had a lot of piglets.
(l) The pain hurt him a lot.
(m) It has helped me a lot.

5

Great, fab, smashing, etc...

Anne was writing about what she had done on the previous night:

> Last night we went to a great disco. I went with a smashing boy. The hall where it was held was super. The sound really was ace. The lighting effects were fab. We all had a great time. It really was cool.

'Oh!' said Miss Madd.

'What's the matter this time?' asked Anne. 'I haven't kept repeating a word.'

'No,' said Miss Madd. 'It's more a question of being attracted to words that are used in everyday speech. There is always one word in fashion to describe something you like very much. Words like: great, smashing, super, ace, fab and cool have all been fashionable in recent years. When writing there are plenty of other words to choose from. Here is a list.'

> lovely   splendid   colourful   good-looking   well-appointed
> sensational   marvellous   stunning   fantastic   brilliant
> perfect   delicious   wonderful   superior   first-rate
> superlative   exquisite   ideal   admirable   glorious   dazzling
> magnificent   attractive   breathtaking   heavenly
> out-of-this-world   stupendous   enthralling   exhilarating

Re-write the above piece by Anne using words from the list.

Then fill in the blanks in this piece. Do not write in the book but copy it out. You may want to use words that are not in the list:

> Last year I went on a ____ holiday to Spain. Everything was ____ right from the start. The plane flight was ____ and an

air hostess served me with a _____ meal.

The hotel was _____ and it was just by a _____ beach. The view from the window was _____. It looked right over a bay. Just a short walk away was a _____ swimming pool.

I thought the night life was _____. There was a _____ disco every night in the open air. We danced till two and had a _____ time.

Now fill in the blanks in these sentences. Once again do not write in the book. It will spoil it for others:

(a) It was going to be a _____ day for fishing.
(b) I am going to get my Mum a _____ present.
(c) It should turn out to be a _____ match.
(d) She is going to move into a _____ house.
(e) The new model from Ford is a _____ car.
(f) I am going to have a _____ Christmas.
(g) The sunset was just _____ .
(h) It really is a _____ picture.
(i) Mohammed Ali was a _____ boxer.
(j) She is a very _____ girl.

6

Big...big...big...

'While we are doing this vocabulary work,' said Mr Wright, 'I thought you might be interested in an early piece of your work, Jim.'

'Oh dear,' said Jim.

'Here it is.'

There was this big woman who lived in a big house on a big hill. She had a big garden with some big trees in it. It must have cost a big sum of money to buy it. She always had a big car standing in the big drive . . .

'It's terrible,' said Jim.

'I'm sure you can improve on it today,' said Mr Wright. 'Here's a list, but there are many other words you can use besides.'

king-size fleshy bulky massive fat monumental
stout obese heavy huge immense overweight plump
enormous vast chubby podgy dumpy mighty
grandiose chunky tubby portly monstrous corpulent
pot-bellied colossal giant gigantic beefy brawny tall
gigantic mountainous outsize oversize excessive large
wide extensive steep formidable great spacious high
fabulous roomy sweeping sizeable muscular

'Some of them have a lovely sound so you can enjoy using them.'

Divide this list into two parts, (a) those suitable to describe people (b) those suitable for things.

Re-write Jim's piece twice using different words for *big* each time. Decide which piece you like the best.

Now improve these sentences:

(a) It was going to be a big occasion.
(b) The village had grown into quite a big place.
(c) There was a big girl on the bus.
(d) He had a big boil on his neck.
(e) The dinosaur was very big.
(f) He sat next to a big boy.
(g) She won a big sum of money on the pools.
(h) There was a big bang and the chimney started to fall.
(i) The big man stood on the corner of the street.
(j) It was a big help to me.
(k) The castle was very big.
(l) She went to live on a big hill.
(m) His hat was too big for him.
(n) The giant could only be described as big.

7

A little bit of . . .

Anne was writing a story to tell her young cousin at bedtime. This is how it began:

A little while ago I saw this little man who lived in a little cave on a little hill. He had a little table outside on which he kept a little saucepan. In the saucepan he had mixed a little bit of goat's milk with a little bit of flour and made little cakes . . .

'What about all the "littles"?' asked Miss Madd.
'I know about them,' said Anne, 'but I was keeping it simple. He is only four.'
'Don't make that mistake,' said Miss Madd. 'Children love words, if they are told plenty of stories. They love big words too. So don't be afraid to use the many other words in the language instead of "little". Here is a list:'

some   tiny   not much   wee   minute   diminutive
miniature   dwarfish   dwarf   slim   slender   meagre   slight
compact   minor   insignificant   petite   dainty   dinky
puny   short   mini   small   low

Make two lists (a) those suitable for people (b) those suitable for things.

Now re-write Anne's story and finish it.

'Before we finish,' said Miss Madd, 'you have used "a bit of". There are alternatives. You will find some in this list and more words for "little".

shortly   soon   cramped   poky   portion of   minute
quantity   a part of   a section of   a morsel of   one or two

23

a piece of   a modicum of   a sliver of   slight   rather   low
some   slightly

Improve these sentences:

  (a) I'll be with you in a little while.
  (b) He lived in a little house.
  (c) She got in a bit of a tangle with the wool.
  (d) There seemed little point in going further down the road.
  (e) Give me a little bit of your chocolate.
  (f) He was a very little boy.
  (g) She only had a little bit of pudding.
  (h) It was only a little mountain.
  (i) The enormous man owned a little cat.
  (j) Will you please give me a little bit of meat.
  (k) I only want a little drink.
  (l) The woman was very little.
  (m) The sugar was kept in a very little jar.

8
Revision exercises

'I think it is time you both did a revision exercise before you forget some of those useful words and phrases,' said Mr Wright.

Do this exercise with Jim and Anne. Improve these sentences:

1 (a) The dress was a sort of greenish colour.
   (b) He sort of turned it upside down.
   (c) I sort of felt the blow to the stomach.
   (d) I think I have a couple of pounds to spare.
   (e) There were a couple of people with him.
   (f) I will see you in a couple of hours' time.
   (g) He went a funny colour when I told him.
   (h) She had a funny look in her eye.
   (i) The funny thing about it was that she was older than Anne.
   (j) The dress had a kind of pleat in it.
   (k) It was not my kind of material.
   (l) I felt kind of sorry for him.
   (m) He was pretty good at football.
   (n) She did pretty well with her cooking.
   (o) He looked pretty silly in that coat.

2 (a) It was a very nice party.
   (b) She had a nice hat on.
   (c) The potatoes tasted very nice.
   (d) There was a nice view from the front window.
   (e) I think he was a very nice man.

These words might help you in Question 3.

repay   bought   hindering   retrieve   receiving   grew angry
becoming   bored   obtain   owned

3 (a) I soon got cross with her.
  (b) It was not as good as the one I had got.
  (c) I got a lot of them in the shop.
  (d) I will get the ball back for you.
  (e) You will have to get him back for that.
  (f) I think you can get better ones than that.
  (g) Why do you have to keep getting in the way?
  (h) I could see she was getting fed up.
  (i) That is not as good as the one I am getting for Christmas.

4 (a) A lot of the saws were blunt.
  (b) I did not really like him a lot.
  (c) There were a lot of people in the exhibition.
  (d) Can I have a lot of pudding, Mum?
  (e) She had really hurt him a lot by not returning his letter.
  (f) There were a lot of elephants in the clearing in the jungle.
  (g) There were a lot of bees round the queen.
  (h) I did not have a lot of hope that we would win the match.

5 (a) She was wearing a really fab outfit.
  (b) I knew it was going to be a smashing party.
  (c) We were going to have a great time.
  (d) I thought the goal he scored was really ace.
  (e) It was a super film.
  (f) The way he played the trumpet was cool.

6 (a) He was a very big baby.
  (b) The wrestler had great big thighs.
  (c) The Eiffel Tower is very big.
  (d) Everest is a big mountain.
  (e) The coat was much too big for him.

7 (a) It only took him a little time to fix it.
  (b) I would only like a little helping, please.
  (c) She really was a very little woman.
  (d) She had a little bit of a cold.
  (e) I am feeling a little ill.

**Now go back through your book. Make two lists (a) words
you already knew but did not use very much in writing,
(b) new words you have learnt to use.**

9
Beautiful and lovely

Anne was writing about her holiday:

> When I went on holiday we went to a beautiful caravan park
> in a lovely valley. From our caravan there was a beautiful
> view of the sea. It was a beautiful blue. The valley was wooded
> and the trees were a lovely green.
> On the beach there were some beautiful girls which pleased
> my Dad. There was one who was so lovely she could have
> been a model. I was envious of her lovely long hair and her
> beautiful legs . . .

Miss Madd looked it over.
'Do you like it?' asked Anne.
'You are overdoing two words,' said Miss Madd.
'I thought you would like this kind of writing,' said Anne.
'But look at "beautiful" and "lovely",' said Miss Madd. 'They
are both useful words. But, as we keep saying, try not to repeat
a word if there are alternatives. Just look at this list. There may
be words you could add to it.

fair radiant pretty sweet paintable stately statuesque
photogenic majestic manly feminine picturesque
scenic exquisite sublime superb excellent grand
gorgeous splendid dazzling magnificent ornate
well-proportioned buxom curvaceous attractive fetching
appealing cute enchanting glamorous shapely pleasant
handsome delightful

Divide this list into two columns, (a) words most suitable to
describe people, (b) words most suitable to describe scenes.
Could some words go in both columns?

Smudge and Chewpen Word Book

Now re-write Anne's piece.

Replace *beautiful* and *lovely* in these sentences:
- (a) He bought her a beautiful watch for Christmas.
- (b) The catalogue was full of lovely clothes.
- (c) The sky was a beautiful red and orange.
- (d) It was a lovely sensation walking through the leaves.
- (e) She lived in a beautiful house in the country.
- (f) She picked him a lovely apple from the tree.
- (g) I think that is the most beautiful film I have ever seen.
- (h) The grandfather clock had a beautiful face.
- (i) I could feel a lovely cool wind on my face.
- (j) She was very cross because she had ripped her beautiful dress.

While you were writing did you think of any other words that were not on the list? Did you want to use *fab, great,* etc.?

Pick five words from the list. Use each one in a sentence of your own making.

10
Nasty!

Anne was writing:

It was a nasty day and I had a nasty cold. My Mum wanted me to take some nasty medicine but I did not want to. As I went out to school I had a nasty shock. There was a nasty accident just in front of me. A dustcart had spilt some nasty rubbish on the road and a motorcyclist had had a nasty skid on it . . .

She took it out proudly to Miss Madd. 'I know what's wrong with this, Miss.'
'Yes,' said Miss Madd.
'It's full of "nasties".'
'You're right,' said Miss Madd. 'Unfortunately there are plenty of words for nasty.'
'Can I have a list?' asked Anne.
'Here it is,' said Miss Madd:

bad vile wretched execrable awful unlikeable
obnoxious beastly horrid ghastly dreadful scruffy
foul rotten lousy putrid sickening revolting
loathsome filthy obscene terrible nauseating
disgusting evil severe violent

Re-write Anne's piece.

Re-write these sentences. You may need words of your own or words from the list.

(a) He crashed with a nasty bang.
(b) The blocked drain gave off a nasty smell.
(c) There was a nasty-looking man outside the pub.

(d) The house was painted a nasty yellow.
(e) The sausage had a nasty taste.
(f) The picture was supposed to be very nasty.
(g) She received a nasty blow to the head.
(h) The pile of rubbish looked really nasty.
(i) He had a nasty pain in the stomach.
(j) She had a nasty fall from her horse.

Now pick five words from the list. Use each in a sentence of your own making.

Now write a paragraph about one of these:

(a) A rubbish dump.
(b) A train accident.
(c) A monster from the sea.

11
Scared with fright!

Jim was just starting to write a ghost story:

> We went into this frightening old house. I was scared stiff. The door creaked behind us and gave me a fright. My brother was scared, too. There were all these scary cobwebs in the room. Suddenly the door slammed behind us. It made us both jump with fright . . .

'Just a minute, Jim,' said Mr Wright. 'I'm sure this is going to be a very good ghost story but you will soon bore your readers, if you use "scare" and "frighten" all the time. Now then I am going to **SCARE** you. I am going to give you an enormous list of words, but they are all useful in writing ghost and horror stories which you do plenty of. Here it is.'

Scare
fear funk stand in awe dread panic start jump
be agitated quake shake tremble quiver shiver blench
wince flinch shrink shy from quail cower dread
give one a turn startle agitate perturb prey on the mind
haunt rattle unnerve put the fear of God into overawe
terrorize terrify horrify harrow chill freeze petrify
make one's blood run cold make one's flesh creep shock

Fright
dread awe cowardice terror panic horror consternation
dismay tremor qualms shivers agitation apprehension

Frightening and Scaring
afraid funky panicky in trepidation in a panic terror-crazed panic-stricken dismayed frightened scared
flabbergasted frozen with terror petrified stunned appalled

31

horrified   aghast   horror-stricken   awestruck   frightened to death   windy   faint-hearted   apprehensive   fearful   haunted terror-ridden   jittery   jumpy   nervy   nervous   cringing fearsome   awesome   horrific   hair-raising   eerie   creepy ghoulish   gruesome   macabre   sinister   ominous   menacing nerve-racking   startling   horrendous

Discuss what these words in this long list mean.

Then write fifteen sentences of your own using words from the lists.

Then improve these sentences:

(a) I was scared about going in to see the headmaster.
(b) He was very scared about going to the dentist.
(c) He was scared when he couldn't stop the sledge.
(d) She was scared when the face appeared at the window.
(e) The tap on the shoulder did give me a fright.
(f) I was filled with fright over the examination.
(g) The cat in the darkness gave him the fright of his life.
(h) The cannibal was very frightening.
(i) The vampire had a most scaring face.
(j) When I clung to the cliff it was the most frightening experience I had had.
(k) I became scared when the engine on the plane failed.

Now go back and complete Jim's story using words from the lists.

12

I like it

Anne was writing about her best friend Tina:

I like going about with Tina. I think it is because we both like the same things. We both like the same pop groups for instance. We also like orange which is our favourite colour. One thing she likes that I don't like, however, is coffee. I can't stand it. I don't see how anybody can like that bitter taste. I only like tea . . .

'Can you see anything wrong with it?' asked Miss Madd.
'It sounds all right,' replied Anne.
'That's because it's so much like speech,' said Miss Madd. 'You have overdone the word "like". It is a useful word but like the word "love" it is overused. Here are some alternatives:

favour   care for   be partial to   appreciate   value   treasure think the world of   admire   revere   adore   be fond of dote on   prize   be enamoured of   be keen on   cherish enjoy   love   relish   prefer

Re-write Anne's piece. Discuss with your friend if any of your replacement words sound phoney. Do you think you should leave some *likes* in?

Try and improve these sentences and then discuss them in the same way.

(a) He did not like going to the dentist's.
(b) I do not like it when you ignore me.
(c) I like to go shopping.
(d) He did not like the way they scored the goal.
(e) She likes her necklace immensely.

(f) She liked him very much.
(g) She liked the way he always noticed her.
(h) The lorry driver liked eggs, beans and chips.
(i) He liked her more than the others.

13

No good

Anne was writing a story for Miss Madd. She showed it to her friend Tina:

> Up till then, Linda had been a good-tempered girl with a good word for everyone. She met Michael and things changed a good deal. She went out with him for the first time on a Friday night and they had a good time together. She thought he was very good-looking. Unlike some of the other boys she had been out with he had good manners.
>
> But after that, it was a good while before she even saw him again. It upset her. She had a good mind to ring him up. But then what good would that do? He ought to contact her. What if he had finished with her for good? No — phoning him would do no good.

'Miss Madd will complain about all the "goods",' said Tina. 'I never seem to learn,' said Anne. 'Ah well, I'll start again.'

Re-write it with Anne. You will find the words and phrases below useful:

> use capable excellent fortunate always strong intention
> fun handsome equable improve things help some
> time extremely considerably praise courteous pleasant
> cheerful kind kindly enjoyable civilised strong impulse
> benefit for ever.

Now improve these sentences without the help of a list:

(a) He made a very good shot at goal.
(b) Our house is a good way from town.
(c) She has always been a very good driver.

(d) They saw a very good film together.
(e) He said that it had been a good holiday.
(f) She was a good help to her mother.
(g) The cake tasted very good.
(h) It was a good thing that he went that way.
(i) He had a good idea about the answer.
(j) The roller coaster was good fun.

Make a list of the words you have used. Compare them with a friend's or with the class.

14

In a bad way

Jim was writing a story about a mountain trip. He showed it to Anne:

It had been a bad day all round. First the weather was very bad. Then he had got that bad cut on his ankle. They were three miles from help down a bad face and track. Their rope had a bad section in it and the food they had brought smelt bad. It would not be so bad if only the mist would lift. No, they were in a bad way . . .

'How funny,' said Anne. 'Tina has just pointed out to me all my "goods". Now I am going to tell you about all your "bads".'
'Oh yes,' said Jim. 'I had better get a list.'
'I'm afraid the list is rather long,' said Mr Wright. 'You will probably have to look some of the words up in a dictionary but I do hope you know some of them. Here it is.'

How many of these words do you know? Discuss them with your teacher:

vile wretched execrable awful worthless shoddy
useless faulty unsatisfactory imperfect incompetent
clumsy foul fetid rotten rank unsound septic
wicked sinful accursed unworthy shameful
scandalous discreditable lamentable deplorable awful
serious treacherous worn unpleasant mouldy pitiable
unendurable intolerable mischievous wanton
outrageous damaging deleterious pernicious disastrous
ruinous calamitous noxious unwholesome poisonous
ominous dreadful evil cursed diabolical

Re-write Jim's piece using some of these words.

Smudge and Chewpen Word Book

Now re-write these sentences:

    (a) It was a bad Monday.
    (b) The doctor looked at his bad hand.
    (c) The witch was very bad.
    (d) I think the bread was bad.
    (e) You are guilty of bad behaviour.
    (f) I think it was very bad the way you let him down.
    (g) The dog was in a bad condition.
    (h) The train disaster was very bad.
    (i) There was a bad smell coming from the drains.
    (j) The shop owner suffered from a bad run of debts.

Write a paragraph about one of these:

    (a) A day of poor weather.
    (b) A casualty ward in a hospital.
    (c) A pop concert you did not like.

15

Old...old...old...

Jim had half-listened as usual. His homework was to write a character study of an old person. He had not listened to Mr Wright's warnings about the word 'old'. Here is the start of his work:

> An old man was going down the street. All the houses in that street were very old. The man's clothes were old, too. He wore an old hat, an old coat and some very old shoes. He carried an old suitcase. It hung from his old hand and bumped against his leg. When he reached the last of the old houses, he stopped and looked up the road. An old cab with an old driver at the wheel was coming along. The old man waved to it. It stopped and he got in lifting his old legs . . .

'Now, Jim,' said Mr Wright, 'let's think about this shall we? We can have "old" for the man but was he a *bent* old man, a *wrinkled* old man or even a *frail* old man? But why "old" again when you come to the houses? Why not *dilapidated* or *tumbledown* or even *timeworn*? And when you come to his clothes what about *well-worn* or *threadbare*? Look here are some words that can help you.'

battered   scuffed   decrepit   ragged   tattered
trodden-down   much-used   gnarled   ancient   antiquated
shaky   out-of-date   tottery.

Re-write Jim's piece using some of the above words.

Here are some more words that mean *old*:

early   primitive   bygone   has-been   expired   retired
antique   archaic   pre-historic   passé   obsolete   superseded

ageing   antediluvian   aged   expired

Now re-write these sentences:

(a) The bicycle was very old.
(b) The old man sat on the step.
(c) He carried a sword of an old design.
(d) He walked in a very old way.
(e) The old tribe lived in a straw hut.
(f) I cannot get you a new part because this one is too old.
(g) Dinosaurs lived in old times.
(h) The woman complained about her old feet.
(i) She gave him a very old book.
(j) The policeman told him that his licence had become too old to be used.

There is another use of *old* as in the sentence: *He was my old mate.* This will be discussed in section 3 of this book.

16

Colours

Jim had written this:

> The view from the headland was marvellous. Across the blue of the bay you could see the white of the cliffs and the rising green hills beyond with their brown ploughed fields like a chessboard. Below was a beach of yellow sand. The red sun was setting and a boat in front of it was silhouetted in black casting a purple shadow on the water. I drank in the beauty of the scene before the grey mist of dusk came upon it.

He sat back and wiped his brow. It had been a real effort. But he really was pleased with it. Mr Wright would love this; it was right up his street — real creative writing.

He was surprised, therefore, at Mr Wright's reaction. 'You have some good ideas in it,' he said, 'and you have a feeling for the scene in front of you. But look at the colours. You would have used those in the primary school. Did you know you can have a car sprayed in 8000 different colours? In fact there are so many they have to use code numbers for some of them because there are not enough names. But let me give you a list of useful colours using the ones you have chosen.'

Red	*Blue*	*Yellow*
rose	azure	canary
coral	steel-blue	gold
russet	sky-blue	primrose
salmon-pink	aquamarine	daffodil
scarlet	midnight-blue	lemon
vermilion	navy	honey
crimson	peacock	gamboge
ginger	turquoise	sandy
rusty	sapphire	straw

Smudge and Chewpen Word Book

Red
brick-red
strawberry

Yellow
ochre

Black
sable
jet-black
ebony
inky
sooty
raven
coal-black
pitch-black

Green
emerald
grass-green
olive
lime

Purple
violet
lavender
amethyst
lilac
puce
plum-coloured
hyacinth

White
luminous
silvery
snowy
frosty
lily-white
pearly
creamy
blond
ivory
bleached

Grey
powder-grey
smoky
ashen
iron-grey
mousy
charcoal-grey
dapple-grey

Brown
bronzed
tanned
brunette
auburn
chestnut
khaki
tawny
maroon
coppery
mahogany
chocolate
coffee

Consult with your art teacher about which shades of colour you do not know.

Now use some of the words in the lists to describe:

    (a) a disco
    (b) a football match at night
    (c) a fair
    (d) the Olympic opening ceremony
    (e) a town seen from a hill

Compare your descriptions with this piece:

> The evening arrived later very beautiful with a rosy flush hovering above the sunset, and passing away into violet and lavender with turquoise green north and south in the sky, and in the east, a great, yellow moon hanging heavy and radiant. It was magnificent to walk between the sunset and the moon, on a road where little holly trees thrust black into the rose and lavender, and starlings flickered in droves across the light.

D.H. Lawrence   *The Rainbow*

17

Comparisons and clichés

Anne was writing another children's story to read at bedtime. She was proud of the way it had started:

> The knight was as bold as brass. His squire was as dead as a doornail after the battle but the knight was as happy as a lark as he rode along that morning. He was as brown as a berry after his return from the Crusades. His armour shone like a new pin. His lance was as sharp as a needle. He knew he was as strong as a horse and that he would rescue the princess from the bad baron as soft as grease . . .

'Oh dear,' said Miss Madd, stopping her, 'your comparisons are all clichés.'

'What are they?' asked Anne.

'A comparison is when we say something is like something else. You have said that the knight was "as bold as brass".'

'I see,' said Anne.

'A cliché is a very common expression in the language. People tend to use them instead of thinking up their own expressions. Good writers always think up their own. You could say, for example, "as bold as an unbeaten warrior" or "as bold as the first man on the moon". Many of these clichés are out of date anyway. Why as bold as brass? Why say "as light as a feather" when you could say "as light as a silicon chip"? Here are some common comparisons which are clichés.'

as bold as brass
as dead as a doornail
as dead as mutton
as happy as Larry
as happy as a lark
as common as dirt

as white as snow
as keen as mustard
as slow as a tortoise
as big as a house
as quiet as a mouse
as swift as an arrow
as thick as a post
as sick as a dog
as brown as a berry
as soft as butter
as light as a feather
as heavy as lead
as thin as a rake
a face as long as a fiddle
as sharp as a razor
as cold as charity
as warm as toast
as sharp as a needle
as bright as a button
as strong as a horse
as weak as a kitten
as brave as a lion

Discuss which of these are old-fashioned.

Re-write them all inventing new comparisons. Try to be different from your neighbour.

as bold as . . .
as dead as . . . etc.

18

Revision exercises

'Time for another revision exercise,' said Mr Wright.

Do these exercises with Jim and Anne. Without looking back try to give five words or phrases with the meaning of:

8   (a) nice
     (b) a lot of
     (c) great, fab, etc.
     (d) big
     (e) little
     (f) beautiful or lovely
     (g) nasty
     (h) scare
     (i) frightened
     (j) like
     (k) bad
     (l) old

Give three words for shades of:

9   (a) red
     (b) blue
     (c) yellow
     (d) black
     (e) green
     (f) purple
     (g) white
     (h) grey
     (i) brown

Improve these sentences:

10 (a) She bought him a beautiful clock for his birthday.
 (b) The sunset was a lovely rose colour.
 (c) She lived in a beautiful cottage.
 (d) It is the most lovely picture I have painted.
 (e) She picked him a beautiful pear from the tree.

11 (a) The racing car had a nasty crash.
 (b) There was a nasty smell coming from the slaughterhouse.
 (c) She had a nasty ache in her side.
 (d) The coat she bought was a nasty pink.
 (e) The pie she had just bought tasted nasty.

12 (a) I was too scared to get on the sledge.
 (b) He was very scared about the interview.
 (c) I was filled with fright about meeting him.
 (d) It was frightening to see the man on the ledge.
 (e) It was very frightening to feel the cobwebs on your face.

13 (a) She did not like going home.
 (b) I like to buy new clothes.
 (c) He liked turkey for Christmas.
 (d) He didn't like having his teeth drilled.
 (e) She did not like the taste of it.

14 (a) There was a very good play on TV.
 (b) The pie tasted very good.
 (c) It is a good while since I saw you.
 (d) The house is a good distance from the station.
 (e) She is very good on a skateboard.

15 (a) The dentist pulled out his bad tooth.
 (b) The king was a bad one.
 (c) The air crash was very bad.
 (d) The food had a bad taste.
 (e) The weather was very bad.

16 (a) The car was very old.
 (b) The suit had become old.
 (c) The woman looked very old.
 (d) The doctor lived in a very old house on the hill.
 (e) The school was a very old one.

17   (a) The coat was a red colour.
     (b) The sea was blue.
     (c) The bird had a yellow colour underneath its body.
     (d) The miner was black as he came up from the pit.
     (e) The trees looked green.
     (f) The heather was a purple colour.
     (g) His hair had turned white.
     (h) He was wearing a grey suit.
     (i) The mud in the marsh was brown and sticky.

Write some new comparisons:

18   (a) as daft as . . .
     (b) as small as . . .
     (c) as green as . . .
     (d) as hot as . . .
     (e) as timid as . . .

Now go back through your book to sections 8 – 17.
Make two lists (a) words you already knew but did not use very
much in writing (b) new words you have learnt to use.

Part two

Word painting

1

The thesaurus

Jim was wondering how Mr Wright could reel off lists of words
so easily. Then he found out. Mr Wright had left his secret
weapon on his desk. It was a book called *Roget's Thesaurus*. In
it there were most of the usual words in English, but they were
arranged differently from the way they were arranged in a
dictionary. They were grouped so that all words of similar
meaning, or synonyms as they are called, all came together.

The beginning of the book put Jim off at first. It started:

Class One Abstract Relations

> Section 1: Existence
> 1. Existence − N existence, ease, being, absoluteness . . .

Jim was lost. It was a good thing Mr Wright came in and found
him. 'Ah,' he said, 'I wondered when we would get round to this.
Do you know that that book is probably more use to you at
your stage of English than a dictionary?'

'I can't make head or tail of it,' replied Jim.

'That's because it is a book you start to use at the back,' said
Mr Wright.

'The back!' exclaimed Jim.

'Look,' said Mr Wright. 'Suppose you are writing about the
sunset and want some colour words other than "red". First look
up "red" in the index at the back. Here we are:

> red
>   revolutionist 149
>   red 431 adj.

'You don't want anything to do with a revolution so it is
"red 431" we are after. Look up Section 431 in the book. Ah,
here we are on page 161:

431. Redness — N redness, flush, blush; fire-glow
417n glow; reddening, warmth, rubescence, rosiness,
ruddiness, bloom, high colour . . .

'You see there is a large list.'

'I don't know what all the words mean,' said Jim.

'You'll find many that you do know. One main use of a
thesaurus is to remind you of a word you've met before but
which you don't use or have forgotten for the moment. You
can always look up words which sound promising in a
dictionary. Now which words in the book might be useful for
writing about a sunset?'

**With Jim look up 'red' in a thesaurus and decide which might
be suitable for describing a sunset.**

After this Jim became more confident with the thesaurus
and started to use it a great deal with his creative writing.
But first Mr Wright gave him an exercise:

Look up these words with Jim:

happy   sad   water   young

Jim couldn't think of the word for the instrument that
measures petrol in a car. He used the thesaurus. Under 466
MEASUREMENT he found: a measure, standard, rule, compass,
callipers, gauge, meter, line, rod, plumb-line, log . . .

Which is the right word to pick?

Here are a few more exercises:

(a) When Jim first saw Mr Wright's thesaurus, he was . . .
attracted, prying, intrigued, curious, inquiring, all agog,
agape, staring?

Which word fits the best?

(b) His voice sounded . . . because the hot, dusty weather had
dried his throat.
dry, anhydrous, arid, undamped, husky, juiceless, siccative?

(c) His boots had given him such blisters that by the end of
the walk he was . . . along.
creeping, lounging, shambling, hobbling, mincing, dawdling,
limping, strolling?

(d) The place where explosives are kept is called a . . .
treasury, pile, rick, museum, repository, magazine,
conservatory, menagerie, aviary, aquarium?

A dictionary might help you check you have the right one.

(e) He stared in terror as the vast army of ants began to . . .
up the hill towards him.
ascend, mount, arise, climb, clamber, swarm, shin, scale,
scramble, aspire?

One or two of these words might be used. Which seems the best?

(f) The two teams were so evenly matched that it was difficult
to . . . which of them would win.
pronosticate, prophesy, predict, presage, forebode,
foretell, soothsay?

2

Choosing the right word 1

When Jim had got the hang of using a thesaurus, he met a
further problem.

'How do you know which word to use?' he asked Mr Wright.
'Sometimes several of them will fit in quite well, when you've
looked them up.'

'It's your own choice,' said Mr Wright. 'Sometimes you
might go wrong. But that doesn't often happen. It's the
feel of the word. You pick one of the shades of meaning.'

'Shades of meaning?' Jim asked.

'Yes. If a lot of words have only slightly different
meanings, you pick the word that suits you best. Try this.'

Mr Wright gave Jim an exercise in choosing words. When
Jim had done it, Mr Wright read it over. He said Jim had not
made any real mistakes. But he felt it could be improved in
places. Jim had always gone for the most difficult word,
trying to please Mr Wright. Mr Wright felt that made the
passage sound a bit pompous.

What would be your version? Try this with Jim.

1.   Jungle

	still		clustered
The jungle was very	hushed	. Trees	crowded
	quiet		thronged
	noiseless		rioted

	hard		stretch
everywhere, making it	difficult	to see for any	space
	impossible		distance

in any direction. The
tops
summits
crests
peaks
of the great trees

joined
met   in
tangled
knots
swags
clumps
masses
of
foliage
leaves
vegetation
which made the light on

the bottom of the forest
floor
ground
dim
dusky
murky
shadowy
. I
crept
shuffled
marched
struggled
along

fighting
battling   with creepers that
wrestling
hindered
impeded
blocked
barred
my way.

2.   Fire

The fire
grew
increased
spread
intensified
. Now it had
ignited
attacked
caught
affected
two other buildings.

The heat from it was
colossal
searing
baking
burning
withering
and the crowd
withdrew
retreated
dispersed
melted away
shrank

from the consuming
leaping
angry
evil
reaching
flames. Another fire engine came
roaring
clanging
bellowing
hooting

up the lane and soon there were more
jets
sprays
cascades
spouts
of water
hissing
falling
arcing
soaring

on to the flames.

3

Choosing the right word 2

It is worthwhile taking care with the words you pick when you are doing your creative writing. Do you take enough care? Mr Wright sets this exercise to help Jim think.

Read this and do this exercise with Jim:

The Meths Drinker
    The <u>down-and-out</u> sat under the railway arches. He looked a <u>heap</u> of <u>verminous</u> rags as he lay <u>sprawled</u> with a bottle of meths in his hand. His hair was <u>matted</u> and the hat on the back of his head had <u>holes</u> in it. He was <u>gazing upwards</u> with <u>reddened</u> eyes waving the bottle. His face was <u>wrinkled</u> and pitted like a <u>walnut</u>. His mouth was <u>creased</u> in a sneer and a <u>cigarette</u> hung loosely from it. Some <u>small</u> children gazed at him and one <u>threw</u> a stone. He <u>whimpered</u> as it <u>hit</u> him. Then he <u>got to</u> his <u>shaky</u> feet still <u>clutching</u> the bottle. The children <u>ran off shouting</u> insults. He <u>shouted</u> back at them showing <u>yellow</u> stumps of teeth.

Look at the underlined words. Has the writer chosen the best words always? Are some of the words below better? Re-write the passage and discuss which is the best version, yours or this one.

down-and-out	destitute, tramp, vagabond
heap	mass, bunch, pile
verminous	flea-ridden, crawling, infested
sprawled	reclined, spreadeagled, flopped
matted	unkempt, greasy, tousled
holes	rips, tears, gaps

gazing	staring, gawping, goggling
upwards	skywards, heavenwards, aloft
reddened	bloodshot, crimson, red-veined
waving	brandishing, flourishing, waggling
wrinkled	creased, lined, crinkled
walnut	prune, old grape, full moon
creased	furrowed, twisted, writhing
cigarette	fag, dog-end, butt-end
small	little, tiny, wee
threw	hurled, chucked, flung
whimpered	whined, groaned, wailed
hit	struck, stung, rapped
got up	rose on, stumbled to, elevated himself to
shaky	unsteady, wobbly, drunken
clutching	grasping, clenching, retaining
ran off	fled, withdrew, retreated
shouting	yelling, hurling, crying
shouted	croaked, growled, snarled
yellow	stained, ochre, jaundiced

Here is another similar exercise. It is about a bombing raid in
the 1939-45 war. Once again has the writer used the best words?
Re-write it using any words from the list you think improve it.
Then discuss which version is best, yours or this one.

The Raid

Alpha Charlie flew towards the streams of orange tracer. The
night was velvet black. Now the searchlights were sweeping
in a criss-cross pattern. The plane weaved to avoid them. The
searchlights were hunting like groping fingers. Suddenly the
bomber ahead was picked out like a thief in the night. The
flak immediately opened up and shells began to burst round
them with a ripping sound. Alpha Charlie shook but was not
hit. Now the target came into its sights. The deadly weapons
plunged down and a line of flashes erupted across the town.
Alpha Charlie immediately turned seeking the covering dark
and the homeward road across the sea.

tracer — bullets that light up when fired
flak — anti-aircraft fire

Smudge and Chewpen Word Book

streams	jets, fountains, rivers
velvet	silky, woven, sable
sweeping	flashing, cleaning, combing
weaved	dodged, zig-zagged, twisted
hunting	probing, questing, seeking
groping	exploring, icy, tentative
picked out	lit-up, illuminated, discovered
thief	murderer, rogue, villain
opened up	commenced, started, broke out
burst	spout, crash, explode
shook	oscillated, vibrated, jerked
deadly	destructive, lethal, fatal
plunged	dived, swooped, descended
erupted	burst, darted, ignited
turned	banked, swerved, altered course
covering	shrouding, concealing, masking
road	flight, journey, path

**Take fifteen of the words you have not used and use them
correctly in separate sentences.**

Finally here is one more similar exercise:

Trapped in the Snow
The day had begun <u>cold</u> but fine. But the wind was in the
east and soon <u>soft</u> grey clouds covered the sun and the first
<u>flecks</u> of snow fell. The journey over the moors was <u>pleasant</u>
in summer but at this time of the year it could be treacherous.
An <u>all-enveloping</u> mist could suddenly <u>form</u> or, as now, snow
could be a <u>danger</u>. She decided to risk it as her mother
depended on her visits. As she <u>reached</u> the high ground the
flakes of snow became the size of <u>butterflies</u> and the wind
<u>drove</u> them horizontally across the narrow road like a <u>white
cloud</u>. It was soon inches deep and drifting. She had still
many miles to go. Then, as she rounded a bend, the car <u>struck</u>
a drift and stuck. She got out but the wind <u>bit into</u> her,
turning her face <u>blue</u>. Visibility was down to almost zero.
She had no shovel. There was <u>nothing for it</u> but to get back
in the car and hope for rescue. The car rocked in the <u>whining</u>
wind like <u>a ship in a storm</u>. Snow <u>blanketed</u> the windows and

58

wind-screen. It soon reached the roof. She was trapped like a
rat in a cage.

cold	freezing, icy, tepid
soft	fleecy, spongy, downy
flecks	flakes, spots, crumbs
pleasant	delightful, agreeable, congenial
treacherous	deadly, perilous, hazardous
all-enveloping	covering, blanketing, smothering
form	appear, take shape, materialize
danger	hazard, peril, menace
reached	gained, attained, made
butterflies	ten p pieces, autumn leaves, blossoms
drove	blew, chased, propelled
white cloud	spume, silver haze, chalky fog
struck	collided with, crashed into, encountered
bit into	lacerated, oozed into, stung
blue	a livid blue, a blotchy blue, purple
nothing for it	no alternative, nothing else, no choice
hope for	pray for, anticipate, trust in
rocked	trembled, swayed, pitched
whining	screaming, screeching, howling
ship in a storm	cork in a pond, leaf in a squall, child on a cakewalk
blanketed	smothered, cloaked, was encrusted on
rat in a cage	miner in a fall, child in a lift, fly in a spider's web.

**Take fifteen of the words you have not used and use them
correctly in separate sentences.**

4

Versions 1

One day Miss Madd put a passage in front of Anne.
'Read that,' she said. 'It's out of a story we read last week.'
'I can't,' Anne objected. 'A lot of the words are missed out.'
'I know,' said Miss Madd. 'It's up to you to put them in.'

Do this exercise with Anne. A list of words to choose from is
given at the bottom of the passage:

'He was about to move on when he gave a cry of fear. In the
light of the street lamp, the beast seemed . . . . Was it only
a dog? The grey shape stood there, looking at him, its tongue
. . . . It had pointed ears and its eyes were . . . . It was . . . .
joined by another and then a third.

Grigg ran with a yell and the wolfish creatures . . . . after
him. A glance showed that they were gaining. In his terror
and the fog, he did not know where he was going. Steps were
in front of him and he . . . . down them. Before he could stop
himself, he was . . . . through mud. He had come to the . . . .
by the river where the tide was out.'

ploughing   lolling   clattered   stealthily   loped   pale
mud-flats   huge

Anne found this quite easy. Did you? Miss Madd gave her
another one. This time she had not read the story before. But
Miss Madd gave her some groups of words to choose from.

Do this with Anne. Pick what you think is the best word. It is
a story about an evil spirit which has haunted a girl. Here the
spirit enters another girl at a bus stop:

                    gloom
In that instant the heaviness left Susan's mind. The evil spirit
                    despair
                    oppression

had gone. She had never been so certain or so happy about

                                        peal
anything in her life before. The bell rang a chime   of victory
                                        symphony
                                        melody

and release and the bus moved on. In the next moment, Susan
    rigid
sat transfixed. The mother had paused at the stop, the better to
    petrified
    frozen.

berate
scold and shake her daughter. A litter-bin rose impossibly from
curse
accuse   turned
its anchorage at the post, upturned itself and descended to cover
                     reversed
                     revolved

the woman's head, cascading banana peel, plastic bags and
crumpled chip papers on her shoulders. On the girl's face was the

              surprise
horror and alarm   of one who feels an unseen presence
              astonishment
         fear

      dry
whose croaking mad voice only she can hear. Then the bus left
      harsh
      grating

them behind.

The words from the original story are given on page 64.

How did yours compare with the original? Which is best?

5

Versions 2

Jim was doing the same kind of exercise with Mr Wright. The first one was based on a Yellow Pages advert.

Do this with Jim. It is an advert in the Yellow Pages directory addressed to advertisers. The words to fill the blanks are at the bottom of the advert.

Yellow Pages

It pays to do _____ through Yellow Pages.

How? Simple. It _____ like this.

Yellow Pages go free to telephone _____ throughout the country.

And when these _____ of _____ buyers want something and they turn to Yellow Pages — they're looking for someone like you to buy from.

Now, put yourself in their _____. Look yourself up in Yellow Pages.

Your name is _____ , but does it _____ out?

If you've got an _____ it does.

It is the _____ that attracts the attention, pulls in the business.

And it works _____ _____ throughout the year.

So it's good business to advertise in Yellow Pages.

Your first move is to ask us for _____ .

Ring your _____ office and we'll tell you all about it.

day-in day-out   details   nearest   business   millions
advertisement (twice)   works   potential   space
subscribers   shoes   there   stand.

Did you find some words easier to fit in than others? Does this teach you anything about language?

This second piece is taken from the Y.H.A. Handbook. Write
your version of it using one of the alternative words. In some
lists is one word which it is highly unlikely to be. Pick out this
word as well. The passage is about advice for mountain walking.

                                        lightly
When you go on the hills, however slightly you regard your own
                                        much

            disregard   convenience
safety please consider   the care   of others and the good
            remember   attitude

                    regional   holidaymakers
name of the Y.H.A. If local   people and other tourists
                    village   trippers

                    minimal
have to rescue you at considerable risk to themselves they will
                    colossal

        nominate   dare-devil   stupid   proud
not believe   you heroic   but merely insane and selfish
        consider   brave   careless   big-headed

                                composition
Boots with mountaineering type plastic soles or nailed boots . . .
                                leather

        useless   comfortable
are essential for easy   and safe hill-walking. Carry gloves,
        necessary   hard

        socks   icy
spare pullovers or wraps. A mountain can be tepid on a summer's
        shirts   cool

                    fully
day. In winter start out adequately clad. Shorts on snow-covered
                    carefully

                freedom   inexperience idiocy
hills are a sign not of hardiness but of naivete and blindness
                toughness   foresight   foolhardiness

Smudge and Chewpen Word Book

Here are the versions the authors wrote. The words are listed in the order they come in the passage:

huge   lolling   pale   stealthily   loped   clattered
ploughing   mud-flats

heaviness   chime   transfixed   scold   reversed
astonishment   harsh

business   works   subscribers   millions   potential   shoes
there   stand   advertisement   advertisement
day-in day-out   details   nearest

lightly   consider   convenience   local   holidaymakers
considerable   consider   heroic   stupid   selfish
composition   comfortable   pullovers   icy   adequately
toughness   inexperience   foolhardiness

6

Sounds

Jim had a good idea for a story. He would have a special agent 008 waiting for someone in a lonely place. He started to work:

> There was no sound except for the sound of the traffic in the distance. It had been a long journey, alone. His mind was still full of the sound of the tyres on the road and the sound of the engine.

Mr Wright looked over his shoulder and said, 'Ah!'. He picked up Jim's book. 'This could be good,' he said, 'but you're missing many opportunities. What sort of sound do horses make?'

'They neigh,' said Jim, thinking it a daft question.

'Notice anything about the word? Notice how it imitates the sound the animal makes to some extent?'

'Yes,' said Jim.

'Well, English is full of words like that. Think of "splash", "groan", "whine". You've used the word "sound" four times so far. What is a word that imitates the sound of traffic?'

Jim thought. 'Hum,' he said.

'Right,' said Mr Wright. 'Start again. Put some sound effects to it.'

'Like "swish" of the tyres on the road?' said Jim.

'That's right,' Mr Wright agreed. 'Get on with it.' He gave Jim his book back.

Jim began again and improved the passage.

Could you improve Jim's piece? Here are a few words that might help.

hum drone murmur drumming thunder whine snarl
growl

Smudge and Chewpen Word Book

Here are some exercises to make the idea clearer:

1 Give one word which imitates the sound these animals make. For instance donkeys *bray*.

frogs	sparrows
geese	owls
eagles	sheep
leopards	mice
snakes	lions

2 Give words which imitate the following sounds:

A wood fire where the wood is wet
Footsteps across very wet and muddy ground
A door slowly opening in a lonely house
A guitar being played badly
Cats late at night
Someone running downstairs
A stream out in the country
Someone running a stick along iron railings
A small child running across a wooden floor

3 Here are some descriptions for you to try. In the first one some words are suggested which can be used as 'sound-effects'.

(a) Bonfire Night
crack fizz hiss crackle whiz hiss snap roar
roar whistle zoom bang crash

(b) A quiet spot out in the country
(c) Inside an engineering factory
(d) Your classroom at this moment
(e) Your classroom at its most noisy
(f) A walk through a zoo
(g) A railway station

Use each of the following words in a separate sentence of your own. All words that imitate sounds are called *onomatopoeic* words.

whisper   screech   babble   cackle   crack   murmur   howl
splash   rustle   clip-clop   buzz   plop   gobble   squelch
crunch   tinkle   tick-tock   clap   pop   gurgle

7

Groupings 1

Jim had been asked to write about a memorable character. He had chosen a thin man he saw daily at the bus-stop:

> To me the man seemed very thin indeed. His face with the fag always stuck in it was so thin you could see the cheek bones sticking through. His wrists were so thin they looked as if they would break if you shook hands with him. I have never seen anybody so thin.

Jim read it. It seemed a good idea for a character. He wanted to stress the man's thinness but it was not quite right. He took it out to Mr Wright.

'Very good,' said Mr Wright. 'This man will make an excellent character. But remember what we told you about repeating words. We have stopped you repeating the common speech words. Now you've used 'thin' four times here. Try not to repeat a word, if there is a better alternative. You could have used "lean", "gaunt" and "emaciated" as well as "thin" here. Don't forget your thesaurus.'

Re-write Jim's piece.

The next day Mr Wright set the class an exercise.

Do it with Jim. Put the following words into their correct places in the sentences. Note how each word is similar yet slightly different from the other words in the group:

(a) surprised   amazed   astounded

The princess was _____ to find a frog in her room. She was _____ when it spoke and _____ when it turned into a prince.

(b) starving   hungry   famished

By the time I had walked seven miles I was _____ . After fourteen I was _____ and after twenty I was _____ .

(c) invisible   indistinct   hazy

The fog came in from the sea to make everything _____ . It thickened rapidly so that the other people near me became _____ . After ten minutes even the lighthouse was _____ .

(d) twinge   ache   agony

He felt a _____ in his tooth as he got into bed. Two hours later it had grown to a dull _____ and before morning he was in _____ .

(e) ruin   damage   havoc

The first wave did severe _____ to the distressed ship, the second wave caused _____ but the third wave brought _____ .

(f) hubbub   whisper   hullaballoo

Two streets away the noise of the crowd was only a _____ . As they drew nearer, they could hear the _____ more clearly and when they came within sight of it they were nearly deafened by the piercing _____ .

With the help of a dictionary and the brilliant Smudge brain Jim did them correctly.

Did you?

Try constructing similar sentences to bring out the shades of meaning in the following groups of words. If you find this too difficult use each word in a separate sentence:

damp   wet   sodden
small   diminutive   microscopic
satisfied   cheerful   ecstatic
fearful   alarmed   panic-stricken
irritable   indignant   furious

8

Groupings 2

Anne had been pleased to begin with. Miss Madd had asked the class to write about a storm. Anne felt she had a great deal to say. But when she looked at what she had written, it didn't seem much good. This is it:

> The wind blew softly at first and then it blew more strongly. It made all kinds of different sounds as it blew in certain places. It blew leaves about. It blew a newspaper across the road. I felt it blow my hair across my face. When I looked up it was blowing the gulls about.

She took it out to Miss Madd and explained how she felt.
'I understand,' Miss Madd said. 'When you do something like this, you are trying to paint with words Have a look at this.'

> 'The wind grew more violent. As the storm went on . . . an invisible colourless thing was trampling and climbing over the roof, making branches creak, springing out of the trees upon the chimney, popping its head into the flue and shrieking and blaspheming at every corner of the walls . . . She had never before been so struck by the devilry of a gusty wind in the wood.'

Thomas Hardy   *The Woodlanders*

Anne read it. ' "Blaspheming" means "cursing God" doesn't it?' she said. 'I couldn't do anything like that.'
'Never mind that,' said Miss Madd. 'Look at the rest of it. Copy it out and underline the words that describe the wind.'

Do this with Anne.

Then Miss Madd said, 'You could try it again. Think of the onomatopoeic words you could use. Here is a list.'

whisper   moan   howl   shriek   creak   clang   wail   sigh
blast

And words like:

gusty   blowy   fresh   squally   boisterous   tempestuous

Write a piece describing a wind in a storm with Anne.

Then try these:

A hot day:
boiling   swelter   flaming   scorching   molten   tropical
torrid   parched   ablaze   sultry   muggy   stuffy   close
oppressive   suffocating   frizzle   bask   sweat   melt

A cold day:
coolness   freshness   zero   iciness   frostiness   chill   shivering
freeze   rime   snow   sleet   fresh   keen   raw   nipping
Arctic   Siberian   perished   blue   wintry   sneeze   shudder

A rainy day:
torrent   torrential   fountain   gush   drizzle   shower
down-pour   drench   soak   cloud-burst   flurry   monsoon
spitting   spout   drip   trickle   splash   flood   inundate
deluge   percolate   pelt

Then read this and write about a misty or a foggy day:

> He crossed some misty meadows by moonlight and the mist lay low
> on the grass, so low that it scarcely reached above his waist, and houses
> and clumps of trees stood out like islands in a milky sea, so sharply
> defined was the upper surface of the mist-bank. He came nearer and
> nearer to a strange thing that floated like a boat upon this magic lake,
> and behold, something moved at the stern, and a rope was whisked
> at the prow, and it changed into a pensive cow, drowsy-eyed, regarding
> him . . .

H.G. Wells   *History of Mr Polly*

How do objects look to you in a fog? What words can you use
to describe them?

9

Groupings 3

'I hope,' said Mr Wright, 'that you have understood that it is not always the big word that makes a piece of writing interesting. It is more knowing the right word to describe something. Very often that right word is a little one. The more words you know the better are you able to pick on the word you need. I want to show you three pieces of writing about the sea. I think you will know most of the words in them, but I wonder whether you would have picked on them to describe the scene as these authors did. Here they are.'

> One evening he and she went up the great sweeping shore of sand towards Theddlethorpe. The long breakers plunged and ran in a hiss of foam along the coast. It was a warm evening. There was not a figure but themselves on the far reaches of sand, no noise but the sound of the sea. Paul loved to see it clanging on the land. He loved to feel himself between the noise of it and the silence of the sandy shore . . . It was quite dark when they turned again. The way home was through a gap in the sandhills, and then along a raised road between two dykes. The country was black and still. From behind the sandhills came the whisper of the sea.

D. H. Lawrence *Sons and Lovers*

> The boy was back now with the sardines and the two baits wrapped in a newspaper and they went down the trail to the skiff, feeling the pebbled sand under their feet, and lifted the skiff and slid her into the water.
> 'Good luck, old man.'
> 'Good luck,' the old man said. He fitted the rope lashings of the oars onto the thole pins and leaning forward against the thrust of the blades in the water, he began to row out of the harbour in the dark. There were other boats from other beaches going out to the sea and the old man heard the dip and push of the oars even though he could not see them now that the moon was below the hills.

Sometimes someone would speak in the boat. But most of the boats were silent except for the dip of the oars. They spread apart after leaving the mouth of the harbour and each one headed for the part of the ocean where he hoped to find fish. The old man knew he was going far out and he left the smell of the land behind and rowed out into the clean early morning smell of the ocean.

Ernest Hemingway   *The Old Man and the Sea*

Laughing on the cliff above the golden beach, we pointed out to each other, as though the other was blind, the great rock of the Worm's Head. The sea was out. We crossed over on slipping stones and stood, at last, triumphantly on the windy top. There was monstrous, thick grass there that made us spring-heeled, and we laughed and bounded on it, scaring the sheep who ran up and down the battered sides like goats. Even on the calmest day a wind blew along the Worm. Above more gulls than I had ever seen before wheeled about and cried shrilly.

Dylan Thomas   *Portrait of the Artist as a Young Dog*

Using some of the words from the examples write about the following:

A walk along the sea shore
A day trip to a seaside resort
A boat trip

10

Said. . .said. . .said. . .

Jim was starting to write another story about his dreaded
Blackgang bunch. Mr Wright looked over his shoulder. This is
what he saw:

'Give me the gun,' said 008.
'Never,' said the Blackgang chief.
'Hand it over at once!' said 008.
'I'll die first,' said the chief.
'That's quite a possibility,' said 008.
'You'd never dare!' said the chief.
'The game is up,' said 008.
'You've a shock coming,' said the chief.
A hand grenade landed at their feet.
'Jump!' said 008.
'Ah! Who's afraid now?' said the chief.

'You've spoilt it by one thing,' said Mr Wright. 'Do you
realise you have ten "saids" in eleven lines of writing?'

'Many writers,' he went on, 'identify the two speakers by
using "said" for the first two speeches like this.'

'Give me the gun,' said 008.
'Never,' said the Blackgang chief.
'Hand it over at once!'
'I'll die first.'
'That's quite a possibility.'
'You'd never dare!'
'The game is up.'

'They omit the "saids". The reader is able to follow because
he knows people speak alternately.
But they also do something else to vary the 'saids'. They use
other words instead.'

74

Said . . . Said . . . Said . . .

Here is a list of the type of words they use:

accused added answered asked bawled begged
beseeched admitted called chortled chuckled croaked
exclaimed gasped groaned growled grinned grumbled
grunted gulped hinted laughed mumbled moaned
murmured muttered ordered requested retorted
shouted snarled sneered screeched sighed squeaked
shrieked sobbed stuttered urged whispered yelled
drawled taunted

Some of these words would group together. For example, *sobbed*
and *cried.* **After discussion, group what words you can.**
Re-write Jim's piece using words from the list.
Do it again using different words from the list. Which piece of
writing do you prefer?
Now use six of the words in separate speeches of your own.

Here is a piece of Anne's that needs help:

'Help me please,' . . .
'What's the matter?' . . .
'My leg is stuck,' . . .
'How have you done that?' . . .
'I slipped and caught my foot,' . . .
'Does it hurt?' . . .
'Very much,' . . .
'Don't cry,' . . .
'I can't help it,' . . .

Invent two people and use words from the list for Anne's piece.

Here is another piece of Jim's. Do the same as with Anne's:

'Let go of my arm,' . . .
'Tell me the truth first,' . . .
'Get off, you swine!' . . .
'You have a lot to tell me,' . . .
'You're hurting me!' . . .
'I mean to,' . . .

75

'All right, I give in,' . . .
'I thought you would,' . . .

Did you or the class think of any other words that could be added to the list when you did this?

11

Said huskily...said sadly...

Anne was puzzling over a piece of writing. 'I understand about using words other than "said",' she said, 'but I can't always find a word that fits properly.'

'Ah!' said Miss Madd. 'What you need to use are adverbs after the "said".'

'What are adverbs?' asked Anne.

'Words that tell us how, when and where something was done,' said Miss Madd. 'Most of them end in -*ly*. Let me show you.'

Look at this with Anne:

'Let me have another helping,' said the boy *greedily*.
'No,' said his mother, *quietly*.
'I'll go to bed at the proper time,' he said *craftily*.
'You'll never learn,' she said *sadly*.

Note how the adverbs tell us how the person spoke.

All the words below are useful adverbs. Copy them out. Group any together that are similar in any way.

bravely balefully craftily croakily encouragingly
faintly forcefully frenziedly gloomily gratefully
greedily gruffly happily hopefully huskily hoarsely
hurriedly moodily openly persuasively readily
quickly quietly sadly slowly spitefully surely shyly
slyly cuttingly certainly insidiously wildly
thoughtfully coaxingly feebly mournfully

Smudge and Chewpen Word Book

Can you add any others to this list?

Use six of the words from the list in separate speeches of your own.
Now do these exercises with Anne:

(a) 'I don't think we'll win,' the captain said _____ .
    'We might,' said the striker _____ .
    'If only we could stop their winger,' said the captain _____.
    'I'm sure we can,' said the striker _____.

(b) 'I don't want to go,' the girl said _____.
    'It will be all right,' said her mother _____.
    'Look what they said last time to me,' the girl said _____.
    'You go, dear,' her mother said _____.

(c) 'I think I can make it,' said the climber _____.
    'You must keep trying,' said his companion _____.
    'I'm about all in,' the climber said _____.
    'There are just twenty metres to go to the ledge,' said
    his companion _____.

(d) 'I'm sorry about my cold,' she said _____.
    'I've got one, too,' said her friend _____.
    'I thought you had,' she said _____.
    'Still, never say die,' said her friend _____.

When writing dialogue you would never use just adverbs with
said but a combination of them and the kind of words used
in Section II. Do the following exercises using a combination
of both methods. You will need to invent the speakers.

(e) 'Can we do it?' ...
    'I'm sure we can,' ...
    'It's going to be hard,' ...
    'Never mind,' ...

(f) 'I've got you at last,' ...
    'What are you going to do?' ...
    'Wouldn't you like to know,' ...
    'You're evil,' ...

(g) 'How funny!' ...
    'Do you really think so?' ...

'It's hilarious,' . . .
'Do it again,' . . .

(h) 'I'm not sure about it,' . . .
'Speak up!' . . .
'I'm doing my best,' . . .
'I can't hear a word,' . . .

May we remind you of the third technique used by writers?
Sometimes they do not use any descriptive words at all to
describe how the speech was said but they leave it to the
reader's imagination. Here is an example:

'I'm going to jump off this bridge,' said 008 slowly.
'You mustn't!' shrieked the detective.
'It's the only way,' laughed 008.
'But what about me?' exclaimed the detective pitifully.
'You'll have to jump as well.'
'What, sixty feet?'
'It's a bullet in the head, if you don't.'
'And a broken back, if I do.'
'That's the choice,' chuckled 008.

Now, using all three techniques, write the following dialogues:

A conversation between two people who do not like getting
up in the morning.
A woman complaining to the manager of a shop
Two boys going down a very steep hill on their bikes
Two people trapped in the snow
A duke telling off his butler for drinking the whisky

12

Revision exercises

'It is time we did a little revising,' Mr Wright told Jim and Anne. 'We will do it by writing about people. Look at these two pieces.'

> I remember him as if it were yesterday, as he came plodding to the inn door, his sea chest following behind him in a hand-barrow; a tall, strong, heavy, nut-brown man; his tarry pigtail falling over the shoulders of his soiled blue coat; his hands ragged and scarred, with broken black nails; and the sabre cut across one cheek, a dirty, livid white. I remember him looking round the cove and whistling to himself as he did so, and then breaking out in that old sea song that he sang so often afterward:
> Fifteen men on a deadman's chest —
> Yo-ho-ho, and a bottle of rum!

R.L. Stevenson   *Treasure Island*

> He was a tiny skeleton, held together by skin and a shiny blue suit. He wore a brown muffler tucked down inside the serge of his suit and I cannot remember his boots — perhaps because I was always looking up at him. He had interesting hands, complicated with knots and veins and brown patches. He always wore a trilby, whether he was sitting by the window or upstairs, or shuffling down the alley . . . or sitting by the counter in the 'Sun'. One remarkable thing about him was his moustache, which faced downwards and seemed of the texture and whiteness of swan's feathers. It covered his mouth and was very beautiful. But even more remarkable, was his breathing, quick as a bird's and noisy, in out, in out, all the time, tick, tick, tick, brittle as a clock with the same sense of urgency and no time to waste, no time for anything else. Over the moustache, under hanging brows on each side of his sharp nose, his eyes looked out, preoccupied and frightened.

W. Golding   *Free Fall*

'Now I want you to go back and look at some of the words we have used and describe a character for me.'

Do this with Jim and Anne. Look at Sections: Part One, 6, 9, 10, 14, 15 and 16; Part Two, 3, 8, 12. Then describe an interesting character you know or would like to put in a story. Note how observant the authors have been. Can you be as observant?

Part three

Registers

1

Avoiding slang

Here is a piece of Jim's early work:

> I copped my eyes on this bloke down the road. He was wearing
> a sort of black bomber jacket. He had a couple of parcels
> under his arms. Probably some things he had pinched. I bet at
> once he was a crook. He had a funny kind of look about him.
> I was pretty sure he was up to no good. You could tell by the
> way the fag hung from his gob. I did not want to tackle him
> because I knew he could duff me up easily. I would have to
> get the fuzz . . .

Jim quite liked it. It was racy. It sounded real. He was
surprised at Mr Wright's reaction.

'This is full of slang,' said Mr Wright gloomily. 'If we are going
to improve your vocabulary you must understand about slang.
Slang is used by people in their everyday speech. It's useful for
quickly conveying thoughts. It can also be picturesque and
funny. But when we're writing we have more time to think about
what we're saying and we can put down our thoughts in a more
exact way. For instance when you wrote 'bloke' did you mean a
fat man, a gaunt man, an unshaven man, a coloured man? We are
inclined to let the slang word mean so many things. Now go
through your story and improve on these expressions.'

copped my eyes   pinched   bet   fag   gob   duff me up
fuzz

**Re-write the story with Jim and improve on the phrases as you
did in Section 1 of this book.**

Smudge and Chewpen Word Book

Here is some slang from the navy in the last war. Can you guess what it means?

> It was our watch for leave so me and my oppo thought we'd have a run ashore in Guzz. We put on our tiddley suits and went down to Aggie Weston's for big eats. I fancied bangers and my winger wanted a tiddy oggie but when we got there they'd run out. I was dead chokker and my oppo had a big weed on about it for the rest of the evening.

Here is a translation of it. How well did you guess?

> It was the turn of our section of the ship's crew to have free time on shore so I and my friend thought we would go to Plymouth. We put our best suits on and went down to a sailor's restaurant for a good meal. I wanted sausages and my friend would have liked a Cornish pasty but when we got there the food was all gone. I was very disappointed and my friend was angry about it for the rest of the evening.

'Closed groups use slang,' said Mr Wright. 'What special school words are there, Jim?'

Does your school have any slang? Make a list.

Now either write a school piece using slang or write about an evening out.

Many common things in our lives have slang expressions for them. For instance, money. Here are some old-fashioned ones. You make a list of modern slang terms for money.

oof   dough   mazuma   spondulicks   ackkers   rhino
readies

Comedians often use slang. They are particularly fond of slang for parts of the body. Here are some:

nose	–	bracket
head	–	bonce
mouth	–	cake hole
foot	–	beetle crusher
ears	–	lugs

86

Which do you find most amusing? How many can you add to the list?

How many slang words do you know for cigarettes?

Now write out these sentences replacing the slang:

(a) My old woman put eggs in the frying pan.
(b) His old man told him off severely.
(c) When I told the teacher the truth he flipped his lid.
(d) Our old gel did her crust when I got in late.
(e) The fuzz were soon on the scene of the crime.
(f) This geezer had a queer look in his eyes.
(g) There were several young birds in the doctor's with kids with runny hooters.
(h) I liked this piece of stuff as soon as I saw her.
(i) I could soon see he was a right berk.
(j) My mother looked at the spuds on the market stall.
(k) I told him to belt up or I would bash his head in.
(l) The burglar stole the sparklers.
(m) Button your lip or it will be the worse for you!
(n) I knew he'd snuffed it when I saw his colour.

Each area in the country tends to have its own slang.
Anne is very interested in cockney rhyming slang. Do you know what these mean?

apples and pears   plates of meat   trouble and strife
tit for tat   Adam and Eve it

Do you know any more?
Do you know any local slang words? Ask your teacher.

'There is one occasion when you can use slang,' said Mr Wright. 'If you're quoting exactly what a character says in your story or play, it's all right. Write a scene in which two criminals discuss dividing up the loot and get into an argument. Use slang to make it real. This should be right up your street, Jim.'

Do this with Jim.

2
Dialect

'Dialect differs from slang in that the inhabitants of a particular area use certain words not often used outside that area. In the old days, when communications between towns and areas were bad, people developed their own words for things. Today many of these words have disappeared or are disappearing as communications have improved so dramatically. The TV and radio also have a great deal to do with the disappearance of dialect,' Miss Madd told Anne.

'What has remained strongly of the old dialects is their accent. Do you know any accents, Anne?'

Write down the names of some accents and dialects with Anne. Here is one to start you: *Geordie*

'Now,' said Miss Madd, 'here is a Lincolnshire dialect poem. Can you guess what the underlined words mean?'

Do this with Anne.

Precautions on the Farm
    Bodge up that 'ooale in the edge, lad
    And stop your mantlin about,
    Just move your grut idle kedge, lad,
    Or them danged owd cauves'll git out.

    Just peg that owd sheep netting down, lad,
    Or the gimmers'll git up to the house,
    Then the missis would half baake me brown, lad,
    And give your young ear a good souse.

Just raightle the pigsty door, lad,
And dooan't let me 'ear so much chelp,
If the sow gits up to the boar, lad,
I'll give your backside a skelp.

Just see that the sneck is fast, lad,
On the door of the deep-litter shed,
I'll swear yar too slow to be last, lad,
I'll do it me dang sen instead.

Just check the electric fence, lad,
Or the cows will git out o' the clooas.
Yar seem that unheppan and dense, lad,
I can tell till I talk messen hoarse.

An' tek the key out o' the car, lad,
I can't let the missis goa out,
She threatens to goa ooame to her Ma, lad,
Then we'd be ewesless heres aboot.

For wi'out her I'd feel nobbut lost, lad,
Altogether she's na'a sa bad,
When I think o' the few bob she cost, lad,
She's the best investment I've had.

                                        Mary Borrows

bodge up	patch up, mend temporarily
'ooale	hole
mantlin	wandering, slouching about
grut	great
kedge	belly
danged	damned
owd	old
cauves	calves
git	get
gimmers	sheep
baake	bake
souse	hit
raightle	put right
dooan't	don't
chelp	backchat
skelp	clout, strike

sneck	catch, fastener on a gate
yar	you're
messen	myself
clooas	field
unheppen	clumsy
tek	take
goa	go
'ooame	home
ewesless	useless
wi'out	without
nobbut	nothing but
na'a	not
sa	so

What dialect words do you know of in your area? Are there any left? What accent do you like the best? Which do you think is the hardest to understand? Is it a good thing or a bad thing that dialects are disappearing?

90

3

Technical words

Jim was in the playground. He was boasting that he could ride a motor bike.

'Easy,' he said. 'You sling your leg over the what's-it and then you kick the doofer on the right hand side. Some bikes don't need this. You press the thingy, instead. At the same time, you twist the what-do-you-call-it on the handlebar and then the motor starts. Then, to move off, you pull on the silver thing in your left hand and you kick down on or you pull up with your toe the thing that sticks out on the left low down. Then you let go with your left hand and you move off.'

Mr Wright who was on playground duty, had been listening, too.

'No one would know how to ride a motor bike from that,' he said.

'What do you mean?' Jim asked.

'Thingy? Doofer?' Mr Wright asked. 'You need to give things their proper names. You needed words like "saddle", "kick-start", "throttle", "twist grip", "self-starter", "clutch-lever", "gear-lever". Anyway, you forgot the most important thing.'

'What was that?' asked Jim.

'You didn't switch the petrol on,' Mr Wright told him and walked away.

Jim didn't like the way Mr Wright had talked to him but he had to admit there was truth in what had been said.

It is important to give things their correct names. It is very important when you are trying to tell someone how to perform a complicated action.

Always learn the correct names of an object.

Here is a diagram of a cassette recorder. All the parts are labelled.
Describe its use to someone who has never used a cassette recorder before.

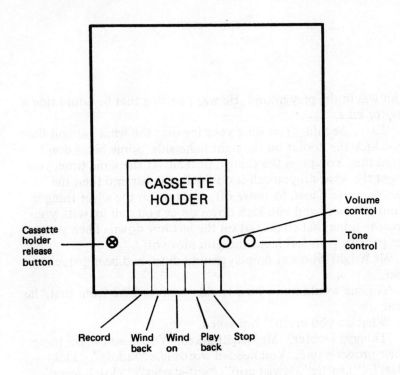

Cassette holder release button

CASSETTE HOLDER

Volume control

Tone control

Record   Wind back   Wind on   Play back   Stop

Here are some words you could find useful:

depress   insert   extract   adjust   power supply   check

Do you know how a motor bike is ridden? Using Mr Wright's terms can you improve on Jim's description?

Alternatively describe how to use a sewing machine. Here are some words to help you:

slide plate   presser foot   thread cutter   needle clamp
needle thread tension   pressure dial   bobbin winder
pattern selector   needle position selector

stitch width selector   stitch length dial
reverse stitch push button   hand wheel
power and light switch   thread   insert   adjust   feed
press   control   guide   regulate

4
Advertising

Advertisers are very careful about the words they choose for adverts. For example:

Moderately-priced garments for the fuller figure.

Means:

Cheap clothes for fat women

The advertiser wants to make his product sound desirable so people will buy it.

'I think many adverts are a swindle,' Jim told Mr Wright.
'If you write some of your own, you might learn something about the technique of advertising,' said Mr Wright.

Go back with Jim. Turn back to part one sections 2, 3, 6, 9 and 12, and make a list of words an advertiser might use. Then make your own adverts using some of these words for:

    a new ice cream
    a seaside resort
    a sports car
    a dress
    a new cigarette
    a hotel
    a kitchen unit

Discuss these adverts and then put them into more normal language:

(a) An exclusive residence in a much sought-after area.
(b) Each Butlin's holiday centre has a galaxy of entertainment.
(c) The suit features an elegantly simple front.
(d) Golden beaches with sun-kissed sands. Send for free brochure.
(e) Tickle your taste buds with this exciting new diet-balanced breakfast cereal.

Many advertisers use technical words to make a product sound exclusive:

World exclusive Microprocessor with Digi-Trim allows you to adjust your watch to five one-hundredths of a second a day.

Does that sound better than:

This special watch has a part in it which allows you to adjust your watch to a twentieth of a second each day?

Write an advert for a tape recorder using technical words.

Then make an advert for a motor bike or sewing machine.

Part four

Additional exercises

1
Slang

Jim gradually improved but he had lapses. Take the time when Mr Wright thought that he had had a good idea. He had asked the class to write a speech for homework. They had to imagine that they were the captain of a team welcoming visitors, or someone making a speech at a wedding or a manager of a firm making a speech to his staff at a party. There were other suggestions but Jim had chosen to be a manager. This is what he had written:

> Well, then, my good old mates, I'm right chuffed to see you all here today. When I take a butcher's round all your friendly mushes, I'm over the moon. It's been a smashing year for the firm and I reckon next year's going to be kind of terrific, too. So, let's sort of sharpen our chompers and get cracking. We'll have a couple of bevvies first and you can all have a good rabbit among yourselves. Then I can promise you a good nosh up and a good do afterwards. That's my lot except to say 'ta' to you all for turning up.

Mr Wright laughed when he read it.
'It's more like a comedian than a manager,' he said.
'Why?' said Jim.
'It's full of slang, for one thing,' Mr Wright told him. 'What made you write it like this?'
'I was thinking of having some mates in for a birthday tea,' Jim said.
'It wouldn't be like that at all,' sighed Mr Wright. 'Now — would it?'
'I suppose a manager would sound more posh,' said Jim.
'Posh?' objected Mr Wright.
'More elegant,' said Jim. He had learned something during the term.

'So — how would he start?' asked Mr Wright.
'Ladies and gentlemen . . . ' Jim began a bit sheepishly.
'And?' Mr Wright prompted him.
' . . . I'm very pleased to see you all here today,' Jim went on.
'You've got the idea. Try again,' Mr Wright told him.
Jim's second version was much better than his first.

Could you improve on Jim's first effort? Write the speech.

Could you write one of these?

A speech to be made at a wedding.
The captain of a team welcoming visitors
Thanking a visitor to the school who has given an interesting
talk
Giving a present to someone who is leaving

**List all the slang words that Jim used in his first version of the
speech.**

2

Sounds

This is part of a poem about a knight in armour, walking among ice-covered rocks:

> Dry clash'd his harness in the icy caves
> And barren chasms and all to left and right
> The bare, black cliff clang'd round him as he based
> His feet on juts of slippery crag that rang
> Sharp-smitten with the dint of armed heels.

Tennyson

The writer has tried to make the words give the sound of metal striking and echoing on rock.

Write a poem on one of these themes. Try to make the words imitate the sounds that you might hear.

A pop concert
A football match
The sounds on the beach on a busy day at the seaside in summer
The sounds of a house where you are alone at night
The noise of a volcano
A village struck by an earthquake
Standing on a bridge over a motorway
The noises you might hear out in wild country in summer
A summer's day by the river
An airport

3

Versions

Anne quite liked choosing words to put into a passage. Here is another example that Miss Madd picked out. Which of the words would you have chosen?

The door was
open
half-open. He knocked and called, knocked and
ajar
called, moving from foot to foot on the
paving
stones
cobbles
of the tiny

yard with his arms
gripped
enfolded
thrust
about him. The house stayed dead

and
quiet
soundless. He shouted again, then
silent
pushed
banged
thrust
the door back

and stepped into a low, white-walled room. Vaguely he
saw
glanced at
noticed

two wooden chairs in front of the fireplace where a thin
fume
frail
spiral

of smoke still rose from the peat, a table and a
ragged
worn
trodden out
strip

of carpet on the floor. In the corner, a curtain made from a

dark-grey
sack
cloth
blanket
was pulled back to
reveal
show
demonstrate
a flight of

ladder-like steps. 'Anyone in?' he cried. There was no answering

                                           twisting

sound of any kind. Shivering, he stood in front of the fire twining

                                                  rubbing

                                 jerk

his hands together until, with a kind of jump he went to the foot

                                           start

                    bawled

of the ladder and called,   'Is anyone there?'

                    raged

                  whispered

Only the wind stirred   outside. He climbed the ladder

                  moaned

Did you get a chance to discuss your choice of words with someone? Here is a list of the words used by the original writer:

ajar   stones   wrapped   silent   thrust   noticed   trail trodden out   blanket   reveal   rubbing   jerk   raged stirred

4

Shades of meaning

'The rain wasn't much at first but it soon got worse and then it got worse still.'

Jim read what he had written. Even he didn't think it was very exciting.

'Shades of meaning, Smudge,' said Mr Wright into his ear. 'Don't you remember the exercise you did?'

Jim shook his head.

'The shower of rain soon became a downpour and after that, very quickly, a deluge,' Mr Wright told him.

'Ah!' said Jim. He remembered.

That night, Mr Wright was busy with the duplicating machine. Next day he set Jim this exercise. Three of Jim's were correct.

Could you do all of them?

Put the following words in their correct places in the sentences:

frozen   cold   chilly

Jim dreamed of being ＿＿＿ but when he felt so＿＿＿ that he woke up, he found himself lying there ＿＿＿ with all his bedclothes on the floor.

baffling   intriguing   puzzling

The problem which at first had seemed ＿＿＿ turned out to be more ＿＿＿ than he had imagined and in the end it was so ＿＿＿ that he had to give up.

plunged   dipped   immersed

The bather ＿＿＿ a toe into the sea and then ＿＿＿ both feet before he ＿＿＿ his shrinking body into the water.

bungler   unskilled   ruined

The workman was worse than _____ ; he was a _____ and he _____ the job completely.

sprint   trot   hurry

He started to _____ when he saw the bus and then to _____ when it began to pull out but he had to _____ to catch it.

garish   colourful   florid

Red shoes with a yellow skirt were _____ enough. Her green jacket made her look too _____ anyway but that purple hat made her look simply _____ .

5

Sports report 1

'What's that you're reading, Smudge?'

Jim jumped and handed over the sheet to Mr Wright. It was a sports report. He had been reading it under the desk. This is what it said:

> Wellingfield who have nose dived so many times this season got a lift on Saturday against Barborough and, it may well be, saved themselves from relegation.
>
> Man of the match was Leggatt. So often off form during the past few weeks, he found it conclusively in the first seconds of the game. Right from the start he was totally in command of the midfield. Time and again he found space. His distribution was unerring and under attack his tackling was beautifully timed.
>
> Even so, Barborough's policy of crowding their area thwarted most of the Wellingfield attempts to strike home. Once a lob forward from Franks gave Johnson his chance but Gartree's header cleared it almost on the line. In the second half, which included the sight of Clement, the referee, felled by Rashley in a collision, Wellingfield had another chance. Anstey, the new Wellingfield striker, facing Butcher, lost possession and the defender turned away deftly and flicked the ball upfield.
>
> Fifteen minutes before time, Wellingfield struck decisively. Anstey, unmarked in Barborough's penalty area, gathered a long ball from Leggatt. This time there was no mistake and he sent a screamer into the net past Sykes.
>
> Barborough pressed hard for the remaining time but failed to equalise and Wellingfield's win seemed well deserved.

'If you can read that, you can read anything,' said Mr Wright.

'Why?' Jim asked.

'It's difficult,' said Mr Wright. 'Look. What does 'nose dived' mean?'

'Lost,' said Jim.

'And "time and again he found space"?'

'He was able to send some good passes to his team mates,' Jim explained.

'If you didn't understand the game, you might find it difficult to read,' Mr Wright commented.

Jim was rather surprised. Mr Wright said no more about it. But Mr Wright had seen his chance. He set an exercise on the passage. The class were not pleased with Jim. But many of them got most of the exercise right. And that included Jim.

The exercise was fairly simple. You had to find simpler ways of saying things.

Could you give simple explanations of all these terms?

relegation
off form
distribution
tackling
crowding their area
a lob forward
header
almost on the line
striker
lost possession
defender
unmarked
penalty area
a long ball
a screamer
equalise

How many other terms do you know that are used in sports reports? You could look at a daily newspaper or your local newspaper. It could help you to make a list.

6

Sports report 2

Mr Wright tried an experiment. He brought in a slightly more old-fashioned sports report. Jim found he could understand that, too, quite well. Here it is:

The pea in the whistle of Jim Blind, the lanky referee from Oldham, had hardly stopped wobbling before United were in action. Jenkins, the Northhampstead nipper, floated over a lovely chip to Boots MacDean who slammed the spheroid against an upright. With Stoppham, the usual lock in the Mudhampton defence, sidelined with injury, the seasiders were panicky from the start. Next Dick Sticks met his brother Chop's pass and split the Mudhampton defence wide open with a peachy one-two with Nix which had Williams groping as if in a black-out as Sticks' cannonball shot stretched the back netting. One nil to United.

The game had hardly restarted before Dawson upended MacDean. The burly Boots twisted in agony as Dawson claimed he had taken a dive. But he quickly recovered to bend a banana shot round Mudhampton's shaky wall. Two nil to United and the crowd was still streaming through the turnstiles ...

Did you find it easy to read? Could you give simple explanations of all these terms?

(a) The pea in the whistle ... had hardly stopped wobbling
(b) lanky
(c) a lovely chip
(d) slammed
(e) spheroid
(f) upright
(g) sidelined
(h) seasiders
(i) peachy one-two
(j) groping as if in a black-out

(k) cannonball shot
(l) stretched the back netting
(m) upended
(n) twisted in agony
(o) taken a dive
(p) bend a banana shot
(q) shaky wall
(r) streaming through the turnstiles.

Your teacher may ask you to criticize these two Sports Reports as examples of journalese.